It was snowing and Nicky was looking for his sledge.

"I've found your sledge, Nicky," said his mum.

Nicky smiled. "Thanks, Mum. Now we can all go sledging tomorrow."

The next day, the friends met at Ranjit's house.

"Let's go to Holly Fields," said Nicky. "The snow will be good there."

"Make sure you are home before it gets dark," said Ranjit's mum. "Ranjit, you look after the bus fares."

Kamal laughed. "This is going to be fun," she said. "I love the snow!"

"Be careful – all of you," said Mum.

The friends waited at the bus stop.

"Here comes Steve," said Nicky. "Perhaps he's going to Holly Fields, too."

"I hope not because I don't like him," said Ranjit.

"Why not?" asked Nicky. "He's OK."

"He's too bossy. Just because he's fifteen."

"You're bossy too!" Kamal told Ranjit and they all laughed.

Steve came up to them at the bus stop.

Adventure in the Snow

by **Pamela Oldfield**
illustrated by **Michael Reid**

Titles in *Springboard* Friends Stage 5

"Are you going to Holly Fields?" he asked. "The hills there are very steep."

"So what?" said Ranjit. "We don't care if the hills are steep."

"It's dangerous so take care," Steve said.

Ranjit was cross. "Don't tell us what to do!"

On the bus, Scruff started to bark.

"Stop it, Scruff!" said Beth.

The bus driver laughed. "Stop it, dog! You make too much noise!"

"Stop barking, Scruff!" said Hope.

"Poor Scruff. He's excited," laughed Nicky.

"So am I, Scruff," said Kamal. "This is our stop. We can get off now."

They got off the bus at Holly Fields. The snow was very deep.

"Let's make a snowman first," said Jamie.

"Let's make snowballs!" said Nicky.

They played in the snow for a long time.
Then they went to the top of one of the
hills. Ranjit put the sledge down.

"Get on behind me, Kamal," said Ranjit.
"You might be scared on your own."

"I won't be scared!" said Kamal. "I'm not going with you."

"The hills are very steep," said Ranjit.

"I don't care! Don't tell me what to do, Ranjit!"

"But mum told me to take care of you!" said Ranjit.

"Don't be bossy, Ranjit," said Hope. "Let her go on her own."

"No!" said Ranjit. "She's got to go with me!"

Suddenly, Scruff saw a black dog and ran after it.

Beth shouted, "Scruff! Come back here!"

"I hope Scruff isn't going to start a fight," said Nicky.

They all shouted at Scruff to come back but he chased after the other dog.

"We'd better go and get him," said
Nicky.

Beth looked worried. "Scruff might get
hurt if there is a fight!"

"Don't worry, Beth," said Nicky. "We'll get
him back."

Ranjit shouted, "Scruff! Come back here!"

They ran after Scruff but Kamal stayed behind. She didn't want to go with the others.

"Good!" she said. "Now I can go down the hill all on my own. Bossy old Ranjit can't stop me! I can do what I like."

But she did feel a bit scared. The hill was very steep.

"Here I go!" shouted Kamal and off she went.

The sledge went very fast. Kamal held on to the sledge. She was very scared.

"Help!" she shouted but no one heard her.

The hill was very steep and very dangerous. Crash! The sledge hit a tree! Kamal fell off into the snow.

Chapter 2

Scruff and the black dog ran a long way. The children were tired when they got to Scruff. He *had* started a fight with the black dog. A man was pulling his dog away.

"Sorry!" said Beth. "Scruff was only playing." She put Scruff's lead on. "You don't want to fight, do you, Scruff?" she said.

But Scruff did want to fight! He began to bark again. He pulled at his lead.

"That's OK!" said the man. "We were just going." He went away with his dog.

The children started to walk back.

"Where did we come from?" asked Hope.

"I think we were over there," said Nicky.

"No, I think we were over there!" said Hope.

Suddenly, Ranjit said, "Where's Kamal?"

They all looked around. Kamal wasn't there.

"Where can she be?" said Ranjit. "Perhaps she's lost!" He was very worried.

Jamie looked around. "She can't be lost, but she might be hiding." He shouted, "Kamal! Where are you?"

They listened but they couldn't hear anything.

"She'd better not be hiding!" said Ranjit. He looked very cross.

"Don't get upset," Hope told him. "That won't help."

"I'll get upset if I want to!" Ranjit shouted. "Don't tell me what to do!"

Hope didn't mind Ranjit shouting. He was worried about Kamal.

Hope started to call Kamal. "Kamal! Where are you? Stop hiding and come out, Kamal!"

Scruff started barking. He started pulling at his lead.

"What is he doing? Is he after that dog again?" asked Hope.

"Stop it, Scruff!" said Beth. "You can't go after that dog again."

She pulled at Scruff's lead.

"We must find Kamal," said Ranjit. "You go that way, Nicky. Ask if anyone has seen Kamal. Hope, you go the other way."

"I'll go up the hills and ask," said Jamie.

They went off to look for Kamal. Beth was still trying to stop Scruff. He looked up at her and barked. Then he pulled at his lead again.

"Stop it!" shouted Beth. "The black dog has gone!"

Beth was scared. It was getting dark.

The others came back.

"I can't see Kamal anywhere," said Hope. "Perhaps she has run off on her own."

"She wouldn't do that," said Ranjit. "She'd be too scared."

"Perhaps she's gone home on her own," said Nicky.

"No," said Ranjit. "She wouldn't do that because I've got her bus fare."

"Here comes Steve," said Hope. "Perhaps he can help us."

Chapter 3

Steve walked up to them.

"You should go home, it's getting dark," he said.

"We can't go home, Steve," said Ranjit. "Kamal is missing. We can't find her anywhere."

Steve looked around.

"Where's your sledge?" he asked. "Perhaps Kamal went down one of the hills on it?"

"I told her not to go down on her own," said Ranjit, "I said it was dangerous."

Suddenly Scruff started barking again and pulled at his lead. Then the lead came out of Beth's hand and Scruff ran off.

"Oh no! Not again!" said Beth.

"Let's go and get him before he gets lost too," said Steve.

Beth and Steve ran after Scruff. The others followed.

Suddenly Scruff stopped. But he was still barking.

"Get him, Beth," Nicky shouted.

"No wait!" shouted Steve. "I think Scruff has found something!"

Scruff stopped barking and it was very quiet. Then they all heard a noise.

"That's funny!" said Hope. "It sounds like someone calling."

"It's Kamal!" said Ranjit. "She's calling for help!"

Then they saw Kamal in the snow, behind a tree. The sledge was broken up.

"We've found her!" cried Nicky.

"We didn't find her," said Beth. "It was Scruff who found her."

Kamal was very upset. She told them what had happened.

"I've hurt my leg. It really hurts to walk," she told them. "And I hit my head when the sledge hit the tree. And the sledge is broken as well."

Kamal started crying.

"I'm very sorry, Ranjit," she said. "You were right. It wasn't safe."

"It's OK," said Ranjit. "I was very bossy. But how can we get you to the bus stop? You can't walk all the way, and you can't go on the sledge."

"Try to hop," said Jamie. "I'll help you."

"I'll try," said Kamal.

Kamal tried to hop. "It makes my head hurt," she told them.

"Poor Kamal," said Beth.

Then Steve said, "Don't worry, Kamal. I'll get you to the bus stop. Help her on to my back, Ranjit."

Ranjit helped Kamal on to Steve's back. Then they set off.

"Look at me, Scruff!" laughed Kamal.

Scruff started to bark but no one was cross with him. They were so pleased that he had found Kamal in the snow.

"Am I too heavy for you, Steve?" asked Kamal.

"No," he told her. "You're as light as snow!"

Ranjit laughed. "That's funny! She must be heavy. She eats so much!"

"I don't eat as much as you!" Kamal told him.

Ranjit laughed again. He was happy that Kamal was safe.

It was dark when they got to the bus stop.

"You must tell your mum what happened, Kamal," said Steve. "Tell her that you hit your head."

"Thanks, Steve, for helping us," said Ranjit.

"Yes, thanks Steve," said Kamal.

"That's OK," said Steve. "Are you all coming back to Holly Fields tomorrow?"

"Perhaps, if the snow hasn't gone," said Nicky.

Steve laughed. "I won't be here tomorrow, so take care!"

"We will!" they told him.

The bus came and they all got on. They gave the bus driver their bus fares.

"Don't tell me that dog has stopped barking!" said the bus driver.

Scruff looked up at him. "Woof!" he said – and he went to sleep.